# Comfort and
# Be Comforted

## Reflections for Caregivers

### Pat Samples

ASSIS
PUBL    .IONS

Comfort and Be Comforted
Reflections for Caregivers
Pat Samples

Edited by Gregory F. Augustine Pierce
Cover design by James Lemons
Typesetting by Desktop Edit Shop, Inc.

Scripture quotations are from the New Revised Standard Version of the Bible, copyright (c) 1989 by the Division of Christian Education of the National Council of the Churches of Christ in the U.S.A. Used with permission. All rights reserved.

Published by:   ACTA Publications
                5559 W. Howard Street
                Skokie, IL 60077
                (800) 397-2282
                www.actapublications.com

Library of Congress Catalog Number: 2001089150
ISBN: 0-87946-223-X  ISBN-13: 978-0-87946-223-9
Year: 15 14 13 12 11 10 09 08 07
Printing: 10 9 8 7 6 5 4 3
Printed in the United States of America

# *Introduction*

If you have picked up this book, someone dear to you is suffering and needs care. You are there with that person—as companion, caregiver and comforter. Whether you care for your loved one at home or offer help from a distance, you are engaged in a great act of love. You are also facing great challenges. Much is being asked of you, yet so much is out of your control. You may long for a little comfort yourself.

The Great Comforter is your constant companion. You are always within easy reach of the arms of God. Surrender your troubles. Open your heart and let in God's love. Trust God and trust yourself as you perform the holy work of caregiving, because it is your calling. Deep within you are the courage, love and wisdom you need to carry it out. Appreciate these qualities inside yourself and tend to them every day. They will grow and bear fruit and nurture you for your mission.

You will not be asked to do more than you can. Nor will you be left alone in giving care. Others will offer to help. Welcome them as visible signs that God is coming to your aid. By allowing their help, you will be able to bring more comfort to your loved one and also get the rest you need to carry on.

May the reflections in this book comfort you. I hope that they remind you to treat yourself gently and give you glimpses into the sacred center of your soul.

# *Persevering Strength*

Where does our strength as caregivers come from? Some days we go beyond what is expected, even beyond what we thought possible. We are there for our loved ones with a power that can topple mountains.

Whatever the weaknesses we've experienced in our caregiving, we've also found a persevering strength we didn't know we possessed. Maybe it comes from pure personal determination or from well-rooted love or from a deep faith. Whatever its source, this newfound strength is a treasure worth preserving.

---

*The Lord is my rock, my fortress, my deliverer.*
Psalm 18:2

# "Stretch" Goals

What kind of caregiver do you want to be? Patient, respectful, flexible, resourceful, strong, faithful, nurturing? Some of these qualities may come easily for you. Others might seem a stretch.

Prayerful attention to your "stretch" goals can help. Focus on one at a time. Ask God for guidance and support. Look for role models in Scripture or in people around you. Remember times when you have acted the way you want to be and practice re-entering the state of mind you were in then.

Remember to celebrate when you succeed in showing your desired qualities. Feel the satisfaction in achieving your goals and offer a prayer of thanks.

---

*I am ready to serve as you would serve, dear God. Show me your way.*

## *The Turbulent Truth*

People often say admiringly, "What a wonderful job you're doing!" This encouraging comment can also cut like a knife.

"They don't understand," we think to ourselves. "I'm *not* doing a wonderful job! And even if I were, I don't *want* to be doing this job. I hate it!"

How can we reveal such nasty feelings to anyone without being judged, patronized or deluged with advice?

It's probably best not to tell most people. They just can't understand unless they are caregivers themselves. But it is important that we do tell someone we trust, someone who will listen with love. A turbulent truth can be poisonous if left to fester without the healing salve of understanding.

---

*We can endure any tragedy as long as we have someone to tell the story to.*

Garrison Keillor

# *Lost and Found*

Nobody provided a map when we become caregivers. When our loved ones get discouraged or uncooperative, we aren't sure what course to take. When we have to make tough choices concerning their care, we find no easy set of directions. We often feel lost.

In a way, we're like Moses, who often felt lost as he wandered for years in the desert. In difficult times, he sometimes forgot that his work was a calling given to him by God and that God was there to guide him on his way. But even when Moses forgot to ask for guidance or doubted God, God was always faithful to Moses. If he lost his way, God would step in and redirect him.

Though we may feel lost as caregivers, God always finds us and brings us safely home.

---

*I once was lost, but now I'm found.*
From the hymn "Amazing Grace"

# *Drained by Worry*

It's easy to care *too much* if you are caring for another. Worry is a sure sign of that basic mistake.

You might insist that there's a lot to worry about! You might even convince yourself that worry is a good thing, a sign of your love. Some caregivers mistakenly think that worry actually *keeps* problems from happening.

But worry doesn't help. It drains and diverts us. As an old song says: "Worry is a rocking chair. You go back and forth and you get nowhere."

Give your worried mind a rest. Ask your wise and loving heart to keep your caring in balance.

-------------------

*When the cares of my heart are many, your consolations cheer my soul.*

Psalm 93:19

# It's a Mystery

The opening of a rosebud is a mystery. How does it happen? The dropping of autumn leaves is a mystery. How can trees appear to die yet blossom again in the spring? The health problems of our loved ones are a mystery too. Why is God allowing all this suffering?

The answers are elusive. We pick roses, rake leaves and wonder. But we can make friends with mystery if we pay attention to it and seek its revelations. What do the cycles of nature have to teach us? What do health challenges reveal about our loved ones, ourselves, life, death, God?

———————————

*Wonderful, Mysterious One, help me to embrace both the revealed and the unknown.*

# *Different Rhythms*

Those we care for are not always on the same timetable we are. We might see that it's time for them to make a change—a new medication, an end to driving the car, perhaps a different place to live.

Our loved ones, however, may have a different sense of timing. They may not be ready to give up the familiar, the comfortable, the sense of control.

Sometimes we must insist; sometimes we must wait. This is a dance, and who takes the lead is not always clear.

---

*Lord of the Dance, let me move easily to your rhythms.*

# *The Great Escape*

There is always some way to escape the stresses and strains of caregiving. TV, working late at our jobs, shopping, the computer, the telephone can all distract us...and oh, do we need to be distracted!

Used as occasional diversions, these activities can delight and refresh us. As a daily well from which to draw sustenance, however, they fail miserably. In fact, it's easy to drown in them—losing ourselves in an obsession that numbs us to our everyday experience.

We can judge the value of our "escapes" not only by the pleasure they give us in the moment but by how well they spark our energy, creativity and openness as we return to the task to which we are called—the care of our loved ones.

---

*Reclaiming the belly laugh can cure a world of woes.*
Jamie Sams

# *Freefalling*

In *Learning to Fly*, author Sam Keen says: "If you can't rise to the occasion, you can always practice falling." He was talking about the art of trapeze flying, but the practice of falling is also an option for those times we aren't up to the demands of caregiving. We can let ourselves off the hook by simply letting go and not trying so hard.

Then we'll realize that—despite our stiff-jawed, unrelenting declarations of "I have to" or "I know I can," sometimes we *can't* will ourselves to do the extraordinary one more time. Sometimes we can't even will ourselves to care that much anymore.

These are the times to back off, respect our feelings of resistance, and cut ourselves some slack.

---

*My Father, if it is possible, let this cup pass from me.*
Matthew 26:39

# *Routine Crises*

One health crisis after another can begin to make trips to the emergency room seem almost routine. But each one wears on our loved ones and saps a little more of our strength as well. We wonder: How serious will it be this time? What new demands will this illness or hospitalization make on us and our families?

We'd like to talk over this new situation with someone, but we don't want to be a burden. We know that others get tired of listening to our concerns.

God's arms, however, are always open.

---

*Cast your burden on the Lord, and he will sustain you.*
Psalm 55:22

# *Keep Dreams Alive*

Unless you're in a health care career, you probably didn't set out to be a caregiver. You had other plans, other interests, other hopes for your life. But now your dreams may have to wait, and even thinking about your own desires may seem selfish when your loved one is suffering so.

Take heart! Caring for another doesn't have to be an either-or thing. Keep your dreams for yourself alive, even if you can't realize them completely right now. Take small steps toward fulfilling them every day—at least in your mind. Treat yourself gently when you can't take greater strides.

Practice kindness toward yourself, and you'll feel more kindly toward your loved one. It's a promise.

---

*Hold fast to dreams, for when dreams go, life is a barren field frozen with snow.*

Langston Hughes

## *Fresh Eyes*

Food, beds, clothing, medicine and the like—ordinary things fill up the days (and nights) of caregivers. Sometimes they seem downright boring. Our loved ones' stillness or snoring can make us depressed or edgy. We dream of winning the lottery...or at least getting a phone call with some interesting news. Anything to break the monotony!

God, give us the fresh eyes and heart of a child, to whom nothing is ordinary. For the child, a stalk of celery becomes a shovel, a canoe, or an airplane. Snores invite giggles, not irritation. Beds become caves or forts or trampolines.

Perhaps monotony is a matter of the mind, not circumstance.

―――――――――

*Nothing is good or bad, but thinking makes it so.*
William Shakespeare

# *It's a Laugh*

Laughing is an "intelligent" thing to do. When we laugh, our brain lets loose a flow of chemicals that send feel-good sparks throughout our whole body. It doesn't even matter whether something funny is actually going on. Our brain takes its cue from the laughter itself and pumps out the endorphins.

Try it. Curl your lips upward and say "ha-ha-ha" fast thirty or forty times. Your belly will loosen, so will your jaws. Keep it going, and soon your whole body will feel lighter. Your spirit will lift. Your heart will open. The strain of caring will ease up.

Plus, who knows? Your loved one might just catch the spirit and join in...or at least ask what is so dog-gone funny. And you can reply, "Nothing, really" or "Everything, of course."

---

*Genuine laughing is a vent of the soul, the nostrils of the heart, and it is just as necessary for health and happiness as spring water is for a trout.*

Josh Billings

# *The Power of No*

Sometimes people ask more of you than you are really able to give. You're tired, you know your limits, yet "the martyr" in you feels obligated to say yes. Then, once you say yes to one more thing, something else is always demanded. There seems to be no end to it...because there isn't.

You can say no, however. Really, you can. In fact, saying no is a fine way to say yes, because by limiting what you do take on, you free your time for what matters most to you and your loved one.

Makes sense, doesn't it? Say yes to what serves and fulfills your priorities. Say no to the rest.

---

*Compassionate Creator, teach me to say no to what may harm me...and ultimately those in my care.*

# *Holding the Hope*

Your loved one might become discouraged, may even "give up" entirely. But the depression of another does not need company. You don't have to embrace it as your own.

Rather, observe it as you would a distant cloud, but keep yourself settled in the sunlight.

Hold out for hope, like an empty vase expecting flowers.

---

*Protect us from all anxiety, as we wait in joyful hope.*
From the Eucharistic Liturgy

# *What You Want*

"What do you want?" Most caregivers, when asked that question, will talk about what they want for their loved ones—health, comfort, rest, peace.

But what do *you* want for *yourself*? Or have you forgotten your own needs and desires? Do you consider them unimportant?

Certainly, those you care for deserve attention. But so do you. God created you out of love and entrusted you with the care of your own life—body, mind and spirit. Treat yourself as the treasure you are.

------------

*Open your hands if you want to be held.*

Rumi

# *No Repair*

When there's a problem, caring people always want to fix it. Yet sometimes we simply cannot. The solution we're sure will work isn't available. Or other people—including those we're caring for—won't cooperate. Or an illness or a situation takes its own course and we cannot do anything to alter it.

We have a choice then. We can tense up and be miserable (and make others around us miserable as well), or we can surrender to our God, who only wants good things for us and only knows how to give good things. We can then open ourselves to what is, trusting that this particular situation is not ours to fix.

---

*So take whatever He gives and give whatever He takes with a big smile.*

Mother Teresa

## *Present at the Creation*

Despite their suffering, those we care for often display great courage. In the midst of grave challenges, they suddenly demonstrate a spark of humor, a burst of strength, a new determination that is truly courageous and exemplary.

We caregivers become witnesses to their heroism.

It's an honor to be present at the creation.

---

*It's easy to invent a life—God does it every day.*
Emily Dickinson

# *The Gift of Mercy*

Every time we judge people harshly—ourselves included—we are diminished. We miss out on the golden gift of mercy.

Mercy is—at its core—an act of generosity. We become larger than our gripes, and we see others as more than their slip-ups. Everyone gets a lift.

When your loved one or a health care provider or a friend or relative does something you consider wrong or insensitive, remember how Jesus forgave the wayward Peter and the woman caught in adultery.

Mercy leaves no scars.

---

*Take heart, son; your sins are forgiven.*
Matthew 9:2

# *A Heart Flush*

Compassion for others prompts us to be kind, and kindness is good for the heart.

As we give comfort to others, we find satisfaction in being able to bring them some relief. A fire of generosity is kindled in us and we are warmed by it. We want nothing in return.

Our heart feels full. We are holding a heart flush.

---

*I am so small I can barely be seen*
*How can this great love be inside me?*

Rumi

# *Asking for Help*

Asking others to help us is a gift to them. Most people want to help. Like a mother needing to release milk from full breasts, they need to release the fullness of their love.

But they can't if we won't let them. By asking for help, we give them a way to express their love, which is a deep desire in everyone's heart.

We also give ourselves a gift. Most importantly, we get the help we need with our caregiving responsibilities. But we also get to practice the "art of gracious receiving." Without our welcome reception, the holy rhythm of giving and receiving is incomplete.

---

*A soul cannot live without loving.*
                                    Catherine of Sienna

25

# *Gifts in the Night*

Nights can be long. Our dear ones may be restless, need frequent help, or just want our company. Or we may be kept awake by our own troubled thoughts, turning them over in our minds relentlessly.

Could we allow nighttime to be a "time of awakening" when sleep will not come?

The night's solemn stillness will minister to us if we let it. In our dark sanctuary, we can patiently await the voice of God.

So be still, dear caregiver. Lay to rest the thoughts of the day. Peace be with you.

---

*Let nothing disturb you. Let nothing frighten you. All things are passing. Who has God wants nothing.*

Teresa of Avila

## *Holy Watchers*

Much of our loved ones' suffering is invisible, at least to the outside world. Sometimes we're the only one who knows the pain is there, where it comes from, and how severe it is. We try to explain it to others, but they aren't around to witness it, day in and day out, the way we are. We stand alone alongside our loved ones as the vessel holding in all the fear and sorrow and hurt.

We are the "holy watchers," the keepers of the flame of love. Some days, just being there as caring witnesses is the most important gift we give.

———————

*Be with me, dear God, as I say to my dear one, "Here I am."*

# *Paying Attention*

Sometimes we have to nudge our loved ones; sometimes we have to hold them back. If they're giving up, we encourage them to keep going. If they're overdoing, we remind them to stop and rest.

Where do we find the balance? When do we step in and say something, when do we step back and let them decide? It takes careful attention to know what to do...and when and how to do it.

It takes respect—for ourselves and for our loved ones.

Prayer helps too.

------------------

*A truthful witness saves lives.*

Proverbs 14:25

# *Useless Mind Chatter*

"I must be doing something wrong." "I should be doing something more." "I'm not the right person for this job."

These are common sentiments among caregivers. But they are traps. Feelings of inadequacy serve no useful purpose and are counterproductive. We can't assume that if only we were doing something more or differently (or were different or better people) things would be substantially better for our loved ones.

This is all useless mind chatter. We would do well to give it over to God and return to the side of the ones we love. That's where our attention is needed.

---

*Powerful, Compassionate One, let me live in your gentle love and stay in the moment.*

# *Our Own Pain*

Watching those we love in pain can be deeply frustrating. We want to free them from their agony. We want to take on their suffering ourselves, our compassion is so great.

Yet it is not our pain. Ultimately, we cannot stop someone else's pain...or even comprehend it, for that matter.

What we can do is acknowledge our own pain—our suffering from watching our loved ones suffer.

Only by being attentive and open to our own feelings can we authentically be present to another's.

---

*It is our work only to understand our own suffering, and, therefore, be available at deeper levels to those we serve.*

Stephen Levine

# *Not Fair*

"All right, God, this is enough. It just isn't fair."

This cry came from a caregiver who could no longer stand to watch his wife suffer. He had tried everything to help her. He was even willing to sell all they owned and move her to another country to get her more promising treatment. When he got word that she couldn't be accepted in the other country's program, however, he was devastated and shook his fist at God.

Yet, at the same time, he clearly longed to rely on that same God for solace.

In the end, he felt God's arms open to embrace both his agony and his anger, and he wept.

---

*Not my will but yours be done.*

Luke 22:42

# *No Big Deal*

Most learning comes from trial and error, so mistakes are the norm when caring for a loved one. You didn't get an instruction book when you signed on as a caregiver. If you forget to give your loved one a medication, if you lose a referral slip, if you say the "wrong" thing, remember that you're in a learning process. Sometimes you will get it right, many times you won't.

No big deal. At the deepest level, your loved one will understand and forgive you.

---

*Don't know about the people*
*but all the scarecrows*
*are crooked.*

Issa

# *Life Itself*

We usually think of people as being active, creative and productive. But if our loved ones have lost these abilities, there is only breathing left.

We caregivers then are left standing beside the essence of life itself.

We are only breathing too.

---

*No man is an island.*

John Donne

# *The Tyranny of Hurry*

Our loved ones slow us down. We must
tend to their needs at their pace, which
means we can't move fast enough to meet ur-
gent schedules—internal or external. We get
impatient, tense up, make demands, lay
blame. Resentment builds.

If we are willing to release ourselves from
the tyranny of hurry, however, we may discover the gifts of going slow, of being present to those we serve on the only timetable
that really matters.

---

*Make haste slowly.*

Suetonius

# Caregiving Rituals

Caregivers need rituals to survive. A small, familiar act can help anchor us when we feel adrift. It may be something as simple as lighting a candle once a day or stopping to meditate for a few moments. We might gather friends and family once a week or once a month and tell stories to or about the loved one who is ill.

One man's circle of friends joined him in the waiting area of the hospital as his wife underwent surgery. They made an "altar" of stones, photos, flowers, and poems, and then they prayed together until she pulled through.

People often ask us how they can help. We can invite them to join with us in a healing ritual.

---

*An altar can be one expression of a concerned heart.*
                                        Jack Kornfield

# *Companion Caregivers*

When our loved ones became ill, everyone rallied to help at first, but only a few people stayed for the long haul. They are the ones who are with us through the long nights, the crises, the endless chores and decisions.

A closeness develops with these special companion caregivers. We cry with them, laugh with them, and sometimes accomplish the impossible together.

The bond we develop with them is a treasure that will always warm our heart.

---

*Gracious God, thank you for those who walk the long road with me.*

## "Favorite Things"

Caring for our loved ones can be all-consuming, if we let it. We can begin to think we have to be doing something for (or at least worrying about) them every moment.

While the demands of caregiving are many, we also need other things to occupy us from time to time. Anything that we enjoy and that absorbs our total attention can be refreshing—from baseball to fishing, from crocheting to playing cards.

These "favorite things" restore our energy and help widen our perspective. They are good in themselves and need no justification. They are a must for caregivers who want to stay sane.

———————————

*Live all you can.*

William James

# *In Appreciation*

When the challenges of caregiving seem too much to bear, you may not think there is much in your life to appreciate. But appreciation is a great antidote to discouragement, so maybe it's worth a try.

Stop a moment and think: Who or what do you value? A best friend? The trill of a canary or the purr of a cat? Perhaps a smile will sneak up on your face. Go ahead, let appreciation fill your heart. It feels so good! You might even make a list of all the things in your life that you appreciate. As the list grows, it may brighten your day and lead to a prayer of thanksgiving.

------

*My soul is satisfied as with a rich feast, and my mouth praises you with joyful lips.*

Psalm 63:5

# *Doing Well*

If you were asked to name the mistakes you've made or the things you've failed to do as a caregiver, chances are you could quickly come up with a long list. But what about those things you are doing well? Could you name them as easily?

Remember: What we pay attention to, grows. If you give your attention to your failures, you will tend to feel bad and stay stuck in doing things poorly. Giving your attention instead to what is going well will help keep your spirits up and your efforts positive.

And the truth is, you're doing a lot well.

---

*Great Encourager, help me remember to feel the satisfaction from giving much.*

# *Friends Who Leave*

While some friends stay the course with us as we care for our loved ones, others don't. They can't tolerate or understand the difficulties brought on by the tasks of caregiving and resent the fact that we aren't available to do things with them as we used to be. They drift away.

We feel as if a part of us has been cut off. Sadness, bitterness, disbelief and resignation overwhelm us.

In time, we discover we cannot hold on to what (or who) is gone. We can only appreciate what has been, and then release it, shedding tears if need be. We then turn for comfort to the one Friend who never leaves.

---

*Come to me, all you that are weary and are carrying heavy burdens, and I will give you rest.*

Matthew 11:28

# The "Chosen Ones"

Our loved ones may prefer to have only certain people take care of them. These "chosen ones" may feel honored or possessive or even resentful, while other family members and friends may feel hurt or jealous or even relieved.

No one is wrong here. Not those who need the care and know who and what they like. Not the chosen. Not the unchosen. All have strong, understandable feelings. All need compassion. Each one has to find a way to make sense of what is happening and choose a fitting course of action.

We caregivers must keep our hearts open to all those involved in the circle of care.

---

*Cultivate a geography of mind where all kinds of souls can bear fruit in the same soil.*

Margot Galt

# *Fear of Death*

Every setback our loved ones suffer can be a scare. Is this latest illness or injury the beginning of the end?

We start to feel on edge. We become watchful, have a hard time sleeping, become alarmed at every cough, every change in breathing that we hear.

Every time we consider the possibility of a loved one's death, we enter the unknown. Control evaporates. Fear surfaces. We don't feel strong enough—or holy enough—to handle these emotions. Again and again, we are given the choice between panicking on our own or trusting the One who is waiting to carry us through.

------------------------

*Fall into the safety of God.*

Rumi

# Rust That Corrodes

Our loved ones don't always appreciate what we do for them. They become irritable, even resistant or abusive. And we may become resentful in response.

But over time resentment becomes rust that corrodes our serenity. The risk of letting it build up is just too damaging.

It helps if we stay focused on our intention—to be loving or to stay calm or simply to keep our loved ones as well as possible—and let their behavior blow by us like the wind. We can also let them know with kind firmness what our limits are and stick to them. Most importantly, we can remember to appreciate ourselves at the end of each day.

---

*We can change our whole life and the attitude of people around us simply by changing ourselves.*

Rudolf Dreikurs

# Old Stories

Stories sometimes reveal the deepest truths about the person you care for.

A photo, a special cup, a piece of jewelry, or some other personal object that has meaning for your loved one can prompt a flood of memories. And then come the stories! Taking time to hear an old tale, as if for the first time, builds the bond between you.

If a story starts to be repeated endlessly and seems a little tired, you might try seeking more richness from it. You could ask with genuine curiosity, "What would you do if that happened today?" or "Every time I hear that story I wonder...." A new story might emerge...and an old one be laid peacefully to rest.

_____

*The party's not over until the stories are told.*
Kathleen Norris

# *The Final Transition*

If your loved one's condition is terminal, the time has come to support him or her through this final transition with love. Yet death is not always easy to talk about.

Prayerful reflection, reading and journaling on death and loss can help prepare you to bring up the subject. You can gently share your thoughts and feelings about death. You can ask, "When you think about dying, what comes to mind?"

Then listen with an open heart. Cry together. Wonder together. Pray together. Make plans together for the end.

God will be close by, cradling you both.

------

*Rock my soul in the bosom of Abraham.*
                            African-American spiritual

# *Skipping School*

We caregivers all know more than when we started about taking care of loved ones. We have learned how to treat bed sores, insert a catheter, find the lowest priced medicines. We certainly know how to fill out insurance forms!

No more new lessons, please!

Maybe it's time to play hooky.

---

*Exercise your right to goof off.*

Anonymous

# *Getaway*

The grass may not be greener on the other side, but at least it's different grass. A periodic night or weekend at a retreat center, a motel, a friend's home, or a campsite—whether near or far from home—is a necessary refresher for caregivers. Occasional longer vacations, if possible, are a good idea too.

For one woman, her monthly getaways became a kind of spiritual exercise. She thought of her time away as a "fast" from her normal routine. She always came back renewed, and closer to God.

Another woman went away for a weekend retreat with her women's group. She laughed her way through the evening hours in this grownup version of a pajama party and slept very late in the mornings. When she returned, she was able to plunge herself back into caregiving with renewed spirit.

------

*He said to them, "Come away to a deserted place all by yourselves and rest a while."*

Mark 6:31

## *Nothing Else Matters*

Sometimes nothing can be done. You do what you can, but you can't make things better.

If there is nothing to do, then do nothing. Just be there. Let go of wishing things were different. Let go of having to do something. Be there as if nothing else mattered, with all your heart.

---

*Be patient towards all that is unsolved in your heart and... try to love the questions themselves.*

Rainer Maria Rilke

# *Sacred Images*

Words can't always convey our sorrow, confusion, exhaustion or despair. A drawing or collage, a sewn or sculptured design may better express the frailty of our heart.

Old family photos, magazine cut-outs, favorite flowers, bird feathers—anything that symbolizes our experience as caregivers can be used to create a personal work of art. Images reveal our story, become our mirror, confirm our reality.

These are sacred images that reflect our experience and raise our spirits. We need to create them, display them, pray over them, and then sit back and let them speak to us.

---

*I decided I was a very stupid fool not to at least paint as I wanted to and say what I wanted to when I painted, as it seemed to be the only thing I could do that didn't concern anybody but myself.*

Georgia O'Keefe

# Car Wash

Did you ever close your eyes while going through a car wash? With the forceful swooshing of water all around you, the slapping and scrubbing of the cleaning machine, and the shaking of the car under all this pressure, it can feel like you're in a hurricane!

Sometimes the pressures of caregiving, with its many demands and the random arrival of bad news, can seem as forceful and unsettling.

In the car wash, as long as we keep the car moving along the track and the windows rolled up, we have nothing to fear. In the same way, if we keep on track with faith and maintain our trust in God, the "noisy" disturbances in our caregiving lives will just wash over us.

---

*Do not let your heart be troubled.*
John 14:1

# *Inspiring Reminders*

Most of us have certain spiritual sayings or quotations that inspire and comfort us: "Let go and let God" or "Not my will but thine be done" or "The Lord is my shepherd," for example. We need to be reminded of these messages when the news about our loved ones' situation is hard to hear or when we are losing patience.

We can find many ways to bring these words to mind when we most need to hear them—posting them on our mirror, dashboard, bedside table, computer or refrigerator; reciting them into a tape recorder and playing the tape while we dress; singing them to a familiar melody or one we create as we ride in the car or take out the trash; sending them in a note or e-mail to a friend.

We don't have to wait to go to church to be uplifted by wise words.

---

*Be still and know that I am God.*

Psalm 46:10

# *Heroic Acts*

When our loved ones are in crisis, we are called on to do things that seem beyond our capacity. We lift them when their weight is beyond our strength. We care for them beyond the point when we'd normally give out. We hold their broken spirit together when it seems beyond repair.

These are acts of quiet heroism. We give our all, out of love, and discover more within us than we dreamed was there. The outcome for our loved ones is not always what we hope, but the act of giving the seemingly impossible is forever embedded in our character. We can celebrate the nobility of what God has given us to give.

---

*I get my strength from God through prayer.*
Mother Teresa

# *Respect and Diplomacy*

Concerned about her mother's slipping health, a woman wondered how to suggest to her that she give up the family home and move to a senior residence. Because her mother had never lived anywhere else, such a change would seem severe and she might not be receptive to the move.

Instead, the woman invited her mother to spend a winter living with her and her family. It was a diplomatic invitation. Her mother got a chance to try out living in a different place while not giving up her own home, and she discovered that she liked the change.

It was a beginning. Each step of change must be negotiated respectfully, honoring the tensions of transitions.

---

*May the God of steadfastness and encouragement grant you to live in harmony with one another.*

Romans 15:5

# *Worth Doing Slowly*

We live in a fast-moving culture, and our lives as caregivers are very full. We fear that if we don't rush all the time we'll never get everything done.

Funny thing is, even when we rush we don't get everything done. And all too often, we make mistakes and step on others' feelings. We add to our stress and diminish our sense of satisfaction.

Everything worth doing is worth doing slowly. Easing up the pace a little can help us stay more relaxed, think more clearly, do things with greater ease and efficiency.

What, really, is the rush?

---

*Timeless One, teach me to move at your pace.*

# *The Ordinary Way*

We clean the dust off the sickroom furniture. We prepare meals and give medications. We help our loved ones move about. The days of a caregiver are ordinary in many ways.

Sometimes this ordinariness is boring. Sometimes it even seems bizarre, as if it cannot be happening to us.

Yet as we tend to the needs of our precious loved ones, the God of love and faithfulness is right there with us, making the ordinary holy and giving it ultimate meaning.

---

*Last time, I think,*
*I'll brush the flies*
*from my father's face.*

Issa

# *Loveliness and Luxury*

When people we love are suffering, we want so much to do something special for them. Beyond the necessary tasks, we want to give them a "day brightener."

A touch of luxury might do the trick! Little niceties such as linen napkins at lunch, beverages served in stemware, an extravagant bouquet, or a trip to a salon for some pampering can restore a sense of loveliness to their lives...and to ours.

Together we can get swept away by moments of beauty and gratitude.

------

*Lavish Creator, let me luxuriate in the gifts you bestow.*

# *Embarrassment*

The loved ones in our care may at times become withdrawn, irritable, even aggressive—leaving little reason for people to like them. Others may even respond to them cruelly, which can break our heart.

We cannot make friends for our loved ones, nor make up for their unfriendly behavior. We may feel embarrassed by what they do at times, but it is important to remember that their behavior is not our fault and we need make no apology for it.

Detaching ourselves from their actions frees us to tend to our own.

---

*There is a balm in Gilead to make the wounded whole.*
African-American spiritual

# *Expanded Patience*

Those we care for may do the most annoying things. They may get demanding, refuse to accept help when they need it, avoid facing their situation.

Yet we love them. At times their quirky ways may even seem endearing. In fact, most likely we will tell fond stories about those very behaviors after our loved ones are gone. Or we may do so already!

So, while our patience is tested, it also expands. We remember that the person before us is a child of God, and our heart softens. We realize that we may need patience extended to us someday...maybe even today.

---

*Suffering produces endurance, and endurance produces character, and character produces hope.*

Romans 5:3-4

# *Money*

Money is a challenge for most caregivers. The services needed by our loved ones are costly. Family members may have to help pay for them or give up their jobs to provide the care themselves.

Trust sincerely that God will provide, giving thanks in advance. Become aware of the many ways God is *already* providing—through money-saving assistance from family, friends, volunteers and community resources. Give thanks.

Also stay alert for new opportunities for income. Be willing to seek and accept more help from others. God cannot give to us if we keep the gates closed.

---

*Generous Creator, thank you for all you have given me...and all that is on its way.*

# *A Few Regrets*

When we watch our loved ones suffering and know there are many things they are no longer able to do, we can be filled with regrets. Should we have gone more places and done more things with them before their health problems got so bad? Should we have done a better job of showing and telling them how much we loved them?

We cannot go back, however, any more than a stream can reverse its course. What we did in the past is over. We must live in the present and go forward from here.

If some regrets linger, it may help to make a list of them. Then, giving ourselves the same mercy God extends to us, we can write after each one: "and I forgive myself."

---

*Because your God is a merciful God, he will neither abandon you nor destroy you.*

Deuteronomy 4:31

# *Repaying the Debt*

Even though we're giving a great deal as we care for our loved ones, we may feel we can never give enough to repay them for all they've done for us over time.

The ones we care for have given generously to us in many ways and continue to do so. They don't do it in hopes of receiving a payback, any more than we do when we are giving to them.

Still, the heartfelt appreciation we feel for our loved ones' generosity helps to fuel our strength when the demands of caregiving get heavy.

---

*A friend loves at all times, and kinsfolk are born to share adversity.*

Proverbs 17:17

# *Take a Hike*

We can hardly think of anything else when our loved ones are in poor health. Our time and attention are occupied with their well-being and their care.

At times, a level of intense attention is required. But we cannot—and should not—sustain it for long periods. We'll lose perspective, along with our sense of humor. Eventually, we'll burn out.

It may be time to take a hike—around the block or at least over to the window. Are there birds singing outside? Children giggling around the corner? Jonquils in bloom in the garden? What other gifts is God offering to refresh us?

---

*The heavens are telling the glory of God; and the firmament proclaims his handiwork.*

Psalm 19:1

# *Take a Nap*

Perhaps no other single activity is so re-freshing for caregivers as a short nap in the middle of the day.

So quit reading this and go do it!

---

*In returning and rest you shall be saved; in quietness and in trust shall be your strength.*

Isaiah 30:15

# *Not Again*

People frequently ask us what is wrong with our loved ones. When we tell them the name of the illness or disability, many respond by launching into a detailed account of what they know about the condition or go into long stories about other people they know who've had it.

None of this helps much, even though we realize that people mean well.

A discussion of the condition itself is not that important to us. What we want to talk about are the particular ways it affects the specific person we are caring for. Friends who can listen to that are like "apples of gold in a setting of silver."

Blessed are those who listen with interest and show compassion. Wise are we if we avoid conversations that drain our spirit.

---

*A word fitly spoken is like apples of gold in a setting of silver.*

Proverbs 25:11

# *Good-byes, Hellos*

Dementia, depression, brain injuries—conditions like these change people's personalities. We feel deeply the loss of their former selves and the change in our relationship.

Tears make sense. We need to say good-bye to the old. One woman, as her husband was slipping rapidly into Alzheimer's, held a small ceremony with family and friends to release and memorialize the way they had always known him.

Change can be frightening, unsettling. We need to honor our feelings of resistance to it. Then, knowing that God wants the best for us, we can trust that under this dark soil of disturbance lies a seed for good...and prepare to water it.

---

*The soul has bandaged moments.*

Emily Dickinson

# *Everywhere*

Our loved ones are with us wherever we go—either in person or on our minds. We may have to take them to the supermarket with us and rely on the stranger behind us to save our place in the checkout line while we help them to the restroom. Or, we may feel anxious every time we get a phone call at work, wondering what new crisis awaits us.

God is with us everywhere too, not only in our hearts but in the hands and hearts of others who assist us. Strangers save that place in line. Co-workers cut us some slack or offer a shoulder to cry on. Professional caregivers provide needed services. Friends and family step in.

---

*Thank you, Everywhere God, for those who shine your love my way.*

# *Household Order*

Household tasks often get neglected as we become absorbed in caring for loved ones. The faucet leaks, unopened mail accumulates, the house gets so messy we don't want to let anyone in.

Life seems chaotic, out of control.

Setting priorities can help restore order. Obviously, the care of our loved ones merits major attention. For the rest, what's critically important? What can wait—maybe even indefinitely? For example, while pride in a clean home is a good thing, if its keeping caring people at a distance then maybe we're missing out on what's most important.

---

*We see a mess, but God sees a message.*
Jessica Hughes

## Caring Their Way

Every time a man with intestinal problems began another round of vomiting, his wife rushed to his side, stroked his back, put a cool cloth on his forehead, and offered words of support. She wanted to show the compassion she felt through her touch and her presence.

After a few times of this solicitous response, her husband pleaded, "Just leave me alone." It was not an angry rebuke, but a clear expression of his desire to have room to handle his own suffering.

Our loved ones' suffering is not ours. There is a delicate balance between showing our concern and being intrusive—or even suffocating. It's important to ask our loved ones what kind of care they find most helpful and then honor their preferences.

------

*Dear God, allow me to know when it's "a time to embrace" and when it's "a time to refrain from embracing."*

# *Honest Feelings*

If our loved ones experience a marked change in personality because of their illness or disability, our feelings toward them can change. One woman, whose husband was affected by a brain injury, said plainly, "I just don't love my husband the same way anymore."

Such stark feelings can startle us. They seem cruel. We feel guilty for having them. Yet hiding from the truth is worse than facing it. By acknowledging our harsh emotions and bringing them into the light, they may more easily dissolve—or be resolved. Even if they don't, owning the truth keeps us honest with ourselves.

Honesty, if we trust it, gives us energy to go on.

---

*Be strong, and let your heart take courage.*
Psalm 27:14

69

## *Busy About Many Things*

When one man's wife developed cancer, he worked hard to keep the house clean and the groceries and meals taken care of. He tended to practical matters because he thought that's what his wife would most appreciate.

Later, she was able to tell him that during her illness what she craved most from him was emotional tenderness. Only then did he realize that he had never even asked her what she wanted. He could also see that his busy activities were a way for him to avoid his own disturbed feelings about her condition.

What do our loved ones really want from us? Have we asked them? What would we feel, if we were willing to feel it?

———————

*Tender Healer, teach me to give to others, heart to heart.*

# *Divine Touch*

We all hunger to be touched. Those we care for certainly do, but so do we caregivers. A hand taking ours, a gentle neck massage, a full-hearted hug—at the right moment each of these can be like rain on parched earth.

When our body and soul ache from the strain of giving care, we can remember to ask a friend or a family member for a tender touch. Our whole being will respond. We will relax, perhaps even to the point of opening up to tears.

We can also soothe our own bodies by gently stroking our own face, neck, arms and legs. Our blood flow will be stimulated, our muscles relieved, our energy restored. We will feel comforted.

The pleasures and power of touch are God-given and glorious!

---

*And he laid his hands on each of them and cured them.*
Luke 4:40

# *Ambiguous Feelings*

You're glad your loved one is coming home from the hospital, but at the same time you hate the thought of all that's going to require of you.

You're scared about having to give shots and help your loved one with bathroom needs, but you expect to muster your courage somehow.

You wish somebody else would take over, but you don't trust anyone else to do it right.

You're sure you'll never make it through this crisis, but you're determined to stay the course.

You're angry at God, but you trust that God will sustain you.

———————————

*Many-faceted God, help me to welcome all my feelings and be at peace with paradox.*

# You Have Permission

When you were a child, you were given permission slips to go places you wanted to go. Parents or teachers had to sign them. Now, you get to sign your own.

If you want to take a break from the constant care of your loved one, the permission has to come from you. Of course, you may need to arrange for someone to fill in while you're away, but you are free to sign the "permission slip" for this to happen at any time and as often as you need.

Remember how glad you were as a child when you got the permission you desired? Give yourself that same happy feeling whenever you're ready for a time out from caregiving.

---

*Christ has set us free.*

Galatians 5:1

# *Ours to Make*

"What if I don't get this right?" This is a big fear for caregivers.

With so much new information to absorb and so many choices to make regarding our loved ones' care, confusion can reign. We fear making mistakes. We may get paralyzed by an inability to make decisions, and then feel guilty because things aren't getting handled correctly. We're waiting for someone to tell us the right thing to do.

No one will. The decisions are ours to make, and make them we must. All decisions are risks. They require trust in ourselves and in God and a willingness to accept our mistakes and human limitations.

---

*God, grant me the serenity to accept the things I cannot change, the courage to change the things I can, and the wisdom to know the difference.*

Reinhold Niebuhr

## Shift into Neutral

Do you ever find yourself caring too much? Have you become so intensely concerned about your loved one's condition that you end up quite tense, worried, exhausted?

That's a good time to shift into neutral gear. Take a deep breath, and as you exhale let all your troubled thoughts drop down into your heart, as though through a funnel. Let them rest there, as you continue breathing deeply. Then, imagine them dissolving. Release your "overcares" and let yourself slip into a restful, neutral state.

---

*The belly should be allowed its deepest breathing, its greatest sigh.*

Stephen Levine

# *Dance Schedule*

Schedules for caregivers can seem worthless. We make plans, and then when our loved ones have problems we make adjustments. Nothing seems to ever work out exactly as we had intended.

What if we were to think of each day as a dance? We would get out on the dance floor, but we would let the beat of the day's music dictate our moves and our timing. The moves of the person we are caring for—as well as those of the other "dancers" around us—would also influence the flow.

Maybe then we could enjoy the twirling and dipping of caregiving a little more. And if we missed a step or two, we'd just laugh at ourselves because it's all in fun.

---

*Let them praise his name with dancing.*
Psalm 149:3

# *Doing Our Best*

We cannot be "the best" at everything. While we are heavily involved in caregiving, we have to let some other things slide a little. We may not be able to be as active at church, call our friends as often, or perform our job as well as we once did.

We cannot even do our "best" all the time for our loved ones, even when their care is our top priority. Sometimes we're too tired or other family members need our attention or we're just feeling "off."

Who says we have to perform at peak efficiency all the time? Not even star athletes do that. Sometimes doing a "fair" job is good enough to let us build up the reserves for when our "best" effort is really necessary.

---

*You can do great things, and never come close to perfect.*

Thom Rutledge

# *Gracious Receiving*

When someone brings over a cake or a bouquet of flowers, we may feel obligated to do something in return.

What if, instead, we simply said, "Thank you, I appreciate it"? Period.

Nothing more is expected. Nothing more is needed. Nothing more, really, is healthy for us if we're in the midst of heavy-duty caregiving.

Kindnesses from others are God's answers to our prayers for help. Let's practice receiving them as we do the sunshine and daffodils—with simple delight.

---

*I am an open vessel, allowing in your blessings, O Lord.*

## *Holy Innocents*

Our loved ones, especially if they have difficult health conditions, can be quite hard to deal with at times. They can be rebellious, ungrateful, disoriented, self-pitying, critical.

It helps to remember that they are innocent. They are doing the best they can at the moment.

Our best response is to continue to give them as much love as we are capable of giving, without judgment or reproach.

———————————

*Love one another with mutual affection; outdo one another in showing honor.*

Romans 12:10

## The Art of Giving

For some of us, giving care comes naturally. We seem to know instinctively what other people need and give it with relative ease.

For others of us, giving care is difficult. We don't seem to know how to help or are reluctant to do so.

The challenge for the "natural" caregivers among us is to avoid over-giving. We've got to resist doing for our loved ones what they can and should do for themselves. We must also leave room for others to contribute to the care.

The challenge for the less skilled givers among us is to open our hearts and approach caregiving with a willingness to learn. By observing what other caregivers do and also by asking our loved ones what would be most helpful to them, we too can learn the art of giving.

---

*Lord, let me give what is mine to give.*

# Changes and Disappointments

As our loved ones become more and more incapacitated, a time comes when we realize we have to let go of some of our own important activities. Because their lives are changing, our lives change as well.

Our moral training tells us we should readily give of ourselves out of love, and of course we *want* to be loving people. Yet the disappointment we feel at having to give up things we value is real. Feeling such loss is not selfish. Pretending we don't feel disappointment would be dishonest.

But disappointment can exist side-by-side with love. In some ways, it ennobles our love as we become more aware of what our caregiving is costing us yet still choose to pay the price.

---

*No one has greater love than this, to lay down one's life for one's friends.*

John 15:13

# *No Strings Attached*

If we caregivers insist we know what's best for our loved ones, we risk their defiant response. We may lose any real opportunity to help them if they resent our unwanted advice.

Advice works best when it is requested and the receiver has agreed to hear it. If we have something we want to suggest to our loved ones, we would do well to ask if they are open to an idea or recommendation. If they say no, we should zip our lips (difficult as that might be) and only speak up if they change their minds. Nor should we insist that they accept our advice once it is given. Their lives are not ours to direct.

We might think of our advice as a gift offered with "no strings attached." Then, if it is rejected or ignored, we won't be offended or disappointed.

---

*Dear God, help me to remember that I am not you.*

# *Divine Physician*

With all the medical care and alternative remedies available today, we caregivers do our best to pursue every possibility to help our loved ones.

Let's not forget the most powerful source of help—someone who has healed those around him time and again. Jesus promised to remain with us through the Holy Spirit, and our faith in him can bring health that goes beyond all appearances.

Let us remember to turn to him in total faith and then trust whatever "medicine" he offers.

---

*I have heard your prayer, I have seen your tears; indeed, I will heal you.*

2 Kings 20:5

# *Cleansing Tears*

As we experience the many sorrows surrounding our loved ones' health problems, our day-to-day grief needs release and validation from others. While we may hesitate to cry publicly, one trusted person or a small group of caring people can become the vessel to receive our tears. Even a good cry alone in the presence of God can have a cleansing effect.

We never need be alone with our sadness or deny our tears.

---

*And God will wipe away every tear from their eyes.*
Revelations 7:17

# Community of Faith

How fortunate caregivers are to have a church community! It is such a comfort when we can get to church to hear the familiar hymns, Scripture readings and messages of hope. Church members feel like extended family.

Even those days we cannot go to church ourselves, we know we are being prayed for. We may also receive visits or calls from clergy and fellow members, especially if we ask for them.

Faith is a fragile thing. Amidst the challenges of caregiving, we can find it hard to keep our faith alive without the ongoing support of our church community. Staying in touch with them reminds us of the hope that comes from being a member of the one body in Christ.

---

*We, who are many, are one body in Christ, and individually we are members one of another.*

Romans 12:5

# *The Caregiver of All*

Whether in desperation or celebration, we can always turn to God. Nothing is too big for God to handle—not our sorrow, nor our anger, nor our anxiety.

Our prayers help us remember that we are one with the Caregiver of All.

---

*To you, O Lord, I lift up my soul. O my God, in you I trust.*

Psalm 25:1

# *What Matters*

When our loved ones are suffering and so much is being asked of us, many of the superficial things that used to matter no longer do. What matters now are the pressing needs of our loved ones and the constant tug on our hearts.

We caregivers spend a lot of time waiting for things to happen. When they finally do, we pay close attention to them because the stakes are so high. We notice how things begin, how they develop, how they come to conclusion. We notice the endings most.

We cling to God, hoping to comprehend the purpose and meaning of it all.

---

*There where clinging to things ends, there God begins to be.*

Meister Eckhart

# *A Touch of Madness*

Some days what comes to mind is committing "murder." We won't do it, of course, but we can get so fed up with our loved ones or with someone associated with their care or with the messes that we have to clean up that we just want to do *somebody* in.

The feeling eventually passes, thank God. Maybe we're able to poke fun at ourselves for the high drama of our rage. We might even take hold of a child's plastic sword and give it a vigorous thrust. Then someone nearby, picking up on our macabre sense of humor, grabs a spatula, crosses swords with us, and proclaims, *"Touché."* Absurdity breeds hilarity, and everyone lightens up.

There's more than one way to "murder" the bad guys.

_____

*I don't cry over troubles*
*Look 'em in the face and*
*Bust 'em like bubbles*

Langston Hughes

# Caregiver Cared For

Our loved ones need lots of emotional and hands-on support. We give it because we care. We give it because we must.

We too need support. Our bodies need relief from tiredness, tension, depletion. Our heavy hearts and sagging spirits could use a lift. Who is there to tend to *our* needs?

A friend, a relative, a nurse, a massage therapist, a counselor—there are many caring people who are willing and able to give us the personal attention we crave. We can ask someone to cook a meal for us, give us a backrub, watch a video with us, read from the Psalms, listen to our sorrow, or just hold us for a little while.

For at least a time, we get to do nothing but receive!

---

*He told his disciples to have a boat ready for him because of the crowd, so that they would not crush him.*

Mark 3:9

# Guilt and Shame

How can we feel angry with our dear ones who are suffering and can't really help what they're doing or saying? Yet our tender-hearted feelings for them can evaporate when we feel pushed to the wall by their behavior.

Then the guilt hits. Our anger seems so self-centered, so un-Christian. Shame nearly consumes us.

When children have temper tantrums, it's usually a sign that they're overtired and overwhelmed. Their loving parents hold them and try to soothe their frenzied spirit by rocking them and offering reassurance. Rather than feeling guilty about our anger, let's offer our troubled spirits some understanding and consolation instead.

---

*Pain is never permanent.*

Teresa of Avila

# *Daily Worship*

Where do caregivers find time to pray, do spiritual reading, even go to church? With all the doctor appointments, laundry to do, baths to give, meals to prepare, who's got time for spiritual matters? We might worry that God will abandon us if we neglect our religious duties.

Not likely. Caring for loved ones is an act of mercy, which is a form of prayer.

When we give care, we are about our Father's business.

---

*Our daily life is our temple and our religion.*
                                        Kahlil Gibran

# *Hanging On*

People naturally want to hang on to the familiar. Our loved ones may resist making a necessary move or giving up a favorite food or activity that is no longer right for them. Caregivers don't necessarily welcome these changes either. We too may want things to stay the same.

But it may be time for our loved ones to get more help than we can give. Or they may no longer have the ability to engage in cherished pastimes. Perhaps they can no longer remember much or control unpleasant outbursts, regardless of how frequent our reminders. We waste energy and do them a disservice if we keep trying to hang on to what is already gone.

We do not have the power to bring back the setting sun.

---

*There is nothing permanent except change.*
Heraclitus

# *Kind Word*

People say such kind things to us as they learn of our struggles with caregiving. Some of their comments settle in like a quiet rain and sustain us for days.

Such a small thing, a kind word.

---

*Be kind to one another, tenderhearted.*
Ephesians 4:32

# *Heartbreak*

If we could take on our loved ones' suffering for them, would we do it? Sometimes we care for them so much, we might even pray for that to happen.

Perhaps what we are really asking for is relief from our own heartbreak. Watching those we care for suffer can seem too much to bear.

Perhaps our heartbreak is an invitation to break open our heart to make room for the more expansive love of God—a love that goes beyond suffering to a satisfying knowledge that all is well at the deepest level of our existence.

———————

*Cast all your anxiety on him, because he cares for you.*

1 Peter 5:7

# What Needs Doing

Fear crops up when we must do things we think we cannot as we care for others. We're afraid of certain unpleasant tasks. For example, we think we can't stand up to family members who interfere, challenge service providers who aren't doing well by our loved ones, accept things we cannot control, make choices we promised our loved ones we would never make.

Drawing on the enduring power of love and compassion, however, we find that we have the strength to do what needs to be done.

We are more courageous than we think.

---

*The Lord is the stronghold of my life; of whom shall I be afraid?*

Psalm 27:1

# *Good Company*

It may come in the middle of the night or when we first arise to face the enormous tasks of the day—that penetrating sense of being alone faced by so many caregivers. No pep talk, no antidepressant pills, no doughnut or sweet roll can take the feeling away. It comes whenever we realize that we have inherited or accepted the main responsibility for the care of our loved ones. No one can possibly understand how heavy that responsibility is or how alone we feel carrying it.

With a slight change in outlook (and in wording), however, we can go from feeling "alone" to feeling "at one" with ourselves... and with God.

Then, we will always be in good company.

---

*This I know, that God is for me.*

Psalm 156:9

# *Miracles*

Jesus tended to the sick with great compassion. People on crutches or in sickbeds sought him out for healing. They knew he could call on the power of God within him to relieve their suffering.

We, too, are compassionate and offer our loved ones forms of healing. Sometimes, through the strength of our faith and the living Spirit of God who dwells in us, our healing may go beyond the expected. A kind of healing takes place we cannot explain by standard measures. Mini-miracles (or even bigger ones) happen through our prayers and effort.

God is at work in us.

---

*Tender, Compassionate One, let me be your instrument for healing, if it be your will.*

# "Cooling Off"

Someone we count on fails to show up for an appointment. A family member criticizes something we've done. Somebody who should know better makes an insensitive remark.

At times like these, we can hardly restrain ourselves. We want to lash out in anger. While offering immediate emotional release, however, the vengeful response usually leaves scars on our soul and harms others as well.

What if we checked in with God before responding, asking in prayer to see the situation through divine eyes? As we still ourselves and turn inward, we already begin to "cool off." We are then more receptive to gentle promptings from God. Who knows, we might be shown a new way to experience relief while practicing mercy.

———————————

*The Lord is gracious and merciful, slow to anger and abounding in steadfast love.*

Psalm 145:8

# *Heart Connection*

Social workers, therapists, specialists, home health aides—so many service providers come and go over the weeks and months. Yet do any of them understand the heartache we feel?

Maybe it would help if we told them about it. It may feel risky, but we can start by revealing just a bit of our heart's story and then check to see if the response we get is also from the heart. If we can make this basic "heart connection," we have a better chance of being in step as we work together in giving care to our loved ones.

If we find someone among the professional caregivers who will go even further and listen attentively to the deepest content of our soul, we will be bathed as if by the grace of God.

---

*Any sorrow can be born if it's put into a story.*
Isak Dinesen

# *Fatigue*

No energy.
Starved for sleep.
Cannot go on.

Stop.
Don't go on.
Rest.

———————————

*God rested from all the work he had done in creation.*
Genesis 2:3

# *True Devotion*

Some caregivers meditate every day. Some do chanting or yoga. Some spend time with God in prayer—alone or with a prayer partner or group. These are all wonderful spiritual practices.

But the care of our ill or disabled loved ones can require our full attention from the time our eyes open in the morning until they close at night...and sometimes half the night as well. Time for devotional activities may seem a luxury.

It helps to remember that caregiving itself is a spiritual practice. Being in loving service—present and open to suffering, to boredom, to whatever comes up in our day-to-day experience—is a holy exercise. When we tend to any child of God, we can rest assured God is right there with us.

---

*Just as you did it to one of the least of these who are members of my family, you did it to me.*

Matthew 25:40

# New Day

Every day with your loved one is a new day. Even if nothing in your circumstances changes much from day to day, you have changed in some way and so has the one you care for.

Yesterday, optimism may have prevailed. Today may seem darker and words of reassurance are needed. Perhaps yesterday neither of you could talk about moving to a different location or mending a severed relationship or getting a will made. But today you might feel ready.

Welcome each new day, ready to meet yourself and your loved ones with fresh curiosity.

---

*We learn through a chain of little incarnations.*
Gerhard E. Frost

# *Allowing Others In*

Nobody said we have to handle all the responsibilities of caring for our loved ones by ourselves. But we might think we're the only ones available or the only ones who will do things right. We may not want others entering our private world.

There are people who want to help, however, and each has something precious to offer. Allowing others in creates a wider circle of care. They share the load, while also receiving the gifts that come from giving. Our loved ones get the benefits of the love and special skills of different people. We caregivers get a breather and feel more able to carry on. We may even learn new ideas from others on how to give better care.

Allowing others in means widening our walls of privacy and trusting others a bit more. Can we ready our hearts to accept the help that God is sending?

---

*Look around you, and see how the fields are ripe for harvesting.*

John 4:35

# A Choice to Serve

Some of the daily tasks of caregiving—emptying a bedpan, for example—can become especially burdensome when we do them with reluctance. It takes extra energy to fight doing what we don't want to do.

What if, instead of resisting an unpleasant task, we were to consciously choose to do it instead? By making it our *choice*, rather than our *obligation*, it can become a free-will "yes" to what God is asking us to do. Then we simply become willing servants, going about our routine, doing what needs to be done.

Once we're no longer giving our attention and energy to fighting the activity, we're also more able to notice some good in it. For example, we might experience gratitude for having a healthy body capable of performing the task.

---

*All that you give me to do, Lord, I accept as my assignment.*

# *Sing a Song*

Throughout history, people have engaged in singing to help them do their work. Workers laying railroad ties eased their labor with rhythmic work songs. Pioneer church women quilting together sang hymns. Mothers still sing lullabies as they care for their babies.

Singing can also ease the strains of care-giving. A familiar melody—or one made up on the spot—can lighten our spirits. If the loved ones we care for join in, all the better.

Burdens aren't so heavy with a song.

---

*It's hard to dislike someone who's singing the same song you are.*

Ellen Kueshner

# *Attentive Listening*

We'd like to say the right thing to ease our loved ones' fears. But finding the right words might be less important than attentive listening.

One man, unable to communicate except with one eyelid, used a blinking code to dictate an *entire book* to a friend who patiently watched for and then verified each communication! Such genuine interest from a supportive listener is what gave the man hope each day and helped keep him alive longer than anyone expected.

We give a great gift and we gain great riches by listening to what others deeply care about.

---

*The first duty of love is to listen.*
Paul Tillich

## *A New Look*

Put on reverse glasses today and look at everything that bothers you about caregiving backwards.

You're running *into* time. Everything is going *right*. You can't *lose*. It's *not* their fault. It's not *your* fault. You've got *plenty* of energy. Everything's so *easy*.

Keep those glasses on for as long as they make you happy.

———————

*Giver of Good, let me see as you would see.*

# *Venting*

Caregivers have to let loose sometimes when the going gets too rough. The tension builds to a point where, if we don't break out, we're going to break apart.

A hearty round of housecleaning can do the job. Sounding off alone in the car might work. Going on a roller coaster ride, watching thriller movies, or whacking at a golf or tennis ball could do the trick.

Let 'er rip!

---

*When the going gets tough, the smart go out for coffee.*
Anonymous

# A Child's View

When you're not sure how to handle a difficult situation with your loved one, ask a child. Or, better yet, watch how children interact with the person you care for.

One little girl, observing a frog in the yard where she played near her ailing and somewhat grumpy grandfather, said, "He's croaky like you, Grandpa!" Everyone, including the grandfather, laughed at this spontaneous honesty. From then on, whenever the man got irritable, the mention of "croakiness" always lightened everyone's mood.

---

*A little child shall lead them.*

Isaiah 11:6

# *Sideways Shift*

Caregiving can seem like a big sacrifice. So much has to be given up. So much has to be gotten used to.

One caregiver said it helped her to think of it as "adjusting," rather than "sacrificing." "Sacrifice sounds more like having to uproot everything," she said. "Adjusting seems more a sideways shift."

Sometimes just using the right word makes all the difference in our attitude.

---

*Something opens our wings. Something*
*makes boredom and hurt disappear.*
*Something fills the cup in front of us.*
*We taste only sacredness.*

Rumi

# *Passing It On*

We are smarter now, we hope, than when we started caregiving. We know more about how the health care system works and how to obtain a variety of support services. We know how it feels to go through the turmoil of change and loss. We know something about taking charge and about letting go.

Around us are others facing what we have faced. They could benefit from our understanding and experience. Caregiver support groups, disease and disability organizations, Internet chatrooms, and church ministries are a few places where we could pass on our wisdom and offer our support.

---

*It is in giving that we receive.*
Prayer of St. Francis of Assisi

# *In Good Hands*

As the day ends, it can be hard for us care-givers to put our minds at rest. Troubling incidents and unfinished tasks from the day often plague our thoughts. Yet we know we need our sleep so we can have energy to care for our loved ones.

To prepare for peaceful sleep, we need to complete our day's agenda. We have two choices about each piece of unfinished business. For some things we can simply make a decision about how and when we will handle the matter later. This gets it moved off today's agenda and off our minds for the night.

All the rest of our concerns, we can turn over to God. We've done what we can about them for today. They will be in good hands while we sleep.

---

*Lord, with your praise we drop off to sleep.*
*Carry us through the night.*

Ghanian hymn